Printed in Great Britain
by Amazon

58875961R00068